FREEDOM

TO BE

Augustus Rains

Augustus has an interest in the philosophy of writers who appear to have knowledge beyond that of the ordinary working person. He looked at religious text and found a questioning, enquiring mind. His belief is that of a universal intelligence surrounding our home planet and every sentient being is a part of it.

It is to this that we return.

To my wife Rose, thank you for kindness and compassion in the nature of love.

Augustus Rains

FREEDOM

TO BE

Published by Amazon

A CIP catalogue record for this title is available from the British Library.

ISBN 9798373065757

Foreword

The following poems are written in a free thinking mind. Free from any dogma, creed, belief system, bias, concept or influences apart from those experienced by and in life itself in this human condition.

Contents   Page

Comments from the author.

From my past and present spiritual experiences I know that I, my true-self, my conscious, my awareness, me, leaves this physical body and that I am very much consciously aware and free from all earthly and worldly things. I am really, truly alive.

In the poem, "What is Free" I question human actions and think, "Human actions. Sad isn't it? They should be free, like you and me"

In the poems, "A Supreme Virtue" and "The Essence of Wisdom" and "The Source of Being" many of the ideas are taken from the teachings of wise masters gone before and I shall be eternally thankful to them.

I Want To Be

I want to be so very kind
Of people's ways to tolerate
In mentality, to be sound
In thinking, to be fortunate

To be gentle in commotions
I want to be considerate
Of people's feelings, emotions
In sufferings, compassionate

I want to be good all round
In all things, in all my doings
In all welfare, on solid ground
And fairness in all my dealings

I want to be pleasant and kind
To folks I meet and say, "Hello"
To be gracious and very kind
To busy people on the go

Life Conditions

There's no God worship condition,
Ritual nor ceremony
There's just kindness and compassion
In life's natural harmony

Just be thankful, just be loving
Let my mind wander in the pure,
The simple and in the giving
In the present moment be sure

To where everything is unowned
And to where everything is freed
Of greed and selfish desired
Possession is liberated

My own true self then freely brings
Realising the whole of nature
Overcome attachment to things
Then in thoughts to become mature

I Care Because

I care not for ritual nor ceremony
I care not for the selfish greed and destruction
But I do care so much for love and harmony
And I do care for the kindness and compassion

In the growing wisdom of this, our human race
Of beings inhabiting this, our planet earth
Who live on seasons gracefully by seasons grace
Seeing the full meaning of earthly life and death

That it is truly not the end of anythings
But truthfully, just merely of transitionings
To greater noble things and greater beginings
Greater noble creations and greater reasonings

Please let me be among the wise in my thinkings
Let me be caring in my deliberations
Let me be wonderfully wise in my doings
Let me be caring in my considerations

Why Bother?

To do so or not to do so
Why do I bother with such things
That give me difficulties so
Perplexings and bewilderings

Is all this part of my growing?
From infancy to adulthood
Are problems part of my sowing?
It would appear from where I'm stood

So I accept it with good heart
Right from the beginnings of life
Can I accept as I then start
Such problems that come with such strife?

I do hope so for all our sakes
That I carry on year on year
Taking life with all its mistakes
And finding new courses to steer

Things do go wrong, of course

Things go wrong as they surely will
Courage, fortitude, clear seeing
I am on the right pathway still
Giving as well as receiving

It is all in the game of life
In the coming, in the going
In the up and down, back and forth
Every which way I am turning

It's never ending its progress
To clear wisdom I may emerge
Wrong thinking, past dogmatic creeds
And passing thoughts I may submerge

So I should bother very much
It keeps me on my pathway sane
Remembering this truth as such
Nothing ventured so naught to gain

Above me, the Cloud

Above me, so many, the cloud
Drifting, forming shapes as they go
And in my life they do so sound
Blowing as the wind doth so blow

No particular way to go
So far or near, so near or far
Forever going to and fro
That is how so many thoughts are

But do then please forgive my all
'Cos I don't know any clear way
The truth is out there standing tall
But I don't have any clear way

So I go on very unclear
What is it I search for next?
Where is it that I go from here?
Why do I seek that so perplexed?

Frustration

A present problem very old
Know how to solve it? Not today
I cannot say, "Stop the world,
I want to get off," I can't say

Frustration comes, like it or not
It is much the way of the world
It be the truth I have not got
So then I drift on like a cloud

Why then so why can I not tell?
What then, what is it I can't see?
How then, how is it can I tell?
And what is it, what is to see?

What is it? All of this madness
Frustration when things go wrong
All of this, it may bring sadness
But sing on like a passing song

Confidence

Angry clouds gather, emotions arise
Greying clouds damping down my confidence
Shouting, "You can't do it. Too small your size.
How dare you show such daring insolence."

And so then I do not do anything
Nothing but cower away in my seat
Confidence shattered and no voice speaking
I resolve myself to one more defeat

What a disaster!!! What a catastrophe!!!
And I feel in my life, just hopelessness
And say, "Will I ever gain this trophy?"
And so a day of dejection, I guess?

Carrying me to more soul searching still
Carrying me to evermore defeat
So nothing changes, nothing ever will
Without courage and will-power complete

Divine Intervention

When things happen and I do not know how
But everything seems to fall into place
Without any of my doing or knowhow
And then I wonder how it all took place

They seem to happen quick, no fuss even
Without thinking or doing anything
Without being of my knowing even
Or any of my doing or thinking

Someone up there is watching it does seem
Looking after me, seeing to my needs
It's not the first time either, it would seem
Things have happened before for my good deeds

Wonderful feelings when it does happen
And what a wonderful result occurs
I be aware, my senses do sharpen
That's how I grow as understanding stirs

Fooled

Most of the people can be fooled
Most of the time they can be fooled
But not all people can be fooled
And not all the time can be fooled

Villains try to fool all the time
Like vipers unawares they strike
Their venomous tongues all the same
Lie after lie pierce like a pike

To deceive and then to fool us
Serving deceit, their selfish blow
Caring not for their victims fuss
They be the lowest of the low

They be the very scum of earth
And for what do they so gain?
No happiness do they beareth
Upon their souls they bear a stain

Adversity

Some conflicts draw us together
And evermore resilient
They make us ever so stronger
Adversity, sometimes silent

Within us, bringing out the best
Of our firm determination.
It must do for there is no rest
Of times that in severe tension

Can and do test to the limit
Our fortitude and endurance
All things to which we do commit
Try our very resilience

And may reduce us to rubble
In our end times when we then go
What of our well fought trouble?
Lost? Gone? If allowed to do so

Learning is Evolving

Reading, writing, arithmetic
Include right and wrong in studies
Learn from writers charismatic
Their wisdom sayings and verses

Take in what I can, absorb it
Resolve my many delusions
Be an integral part of it
Come to many right conclusions

Modify thoughts going along
Change, enhance my thinking nature
My senses of right and of wrong
Of good and bad, of my honour

Analyse, question all the lot
Sense and nonsense the very same
Out of nonsense clarity got
On reaching my stage in life's game

Going with the Flow

In a state of flux flows matter
Nothing ever stays the same gauge
And nothing fixed then does scatter
Everything in a state of change

Living too, in constant moving
Ever changing, to forming new
Old dwindles away, it's ever changing
Ever moving, old leads to new

To survive, life must evolve too
Stagnation will dull the spirit
So on it must move, it must do
Inventiveness, just get on it

To improve our welfare being
Our living for all, not just some
That's life in the very making
Children, generations to come

The Essence of Wisdom

From whence I cometh? I want to know this
I think now it would be wise to know this
What is? What is not? What is beyond this?
I want to find all knowledge such as this

Where shall I be going? To know, just how?
And where do I start my searching? And how?
Realise who I am, know me, just how?
Know my own senses, my spirit And how?

What kind is beyond existence? Just what?
What kind of life am I having? Just what?
What kind of strife in the future? Just what?
What kind of this and that and where. Just what?

But do I need to know such things? And why?
To realise my own wisdom? But why?
Even begin to think this way? And why?
Is this the essence of wisdom? But why?

The Source of Being

Why can I not just remain happily
Going on my merry way? Happily
Not a care in the world, be happily
Living life to the fullest. Happily

Why? Why not? Why can it not be that way?
Why can't life be a much simpler way?
Of full living in a safe and sound way
Will the world allow it to be that way?

Someday it might just do that. Why not now?
Has there to be conflict? Why not peace now?
The earth has resources for all, right now
Can it be for all peoples to care, now?

I don't know the very source of being
I don't know what is beyond being
I think it must be a happy being
Is then happiness the source of being?

The Clock Ticks On

And does give routine in my life
It does not cease to take control
Of my working ways and my strife
If it did not I would then strole

Along my own living life's way
Slowly, maybe without purpose
Mostly an easy sort of way
Without anything to compose

Perhaps it would be so joyful
To go along my joyful way
Fulfilling a purpose joyful
Perhaps then find a wisdom way

With ease and a tranquillity
No worries, no cares, only joy
Perhaps I might find quality
If a new way I might employ

Time to Let Go

To let go of so much clutter
In my dealings, in my doings
That causes my life to flutter
In my comings, in my goings

And to try to do of much else
Presents problems, complications
So it be to let go with ease
These are of the best solutions

Let go of things that do not work
Relationships that have outgrown
Friendships moving on spent-up talk
If loving has moved on and flown

Even let go of earthly things
And when the spirit takes over
From that of our future doings
With earthly things given over

The Value of a Smile

Life is like a merry-go-round
With music, a wonderful sound
Up and down does it go around
So do not fall off to the ground

Keep smiling at life, my tutor
Create happiness, my belief
Full of promise for my future
There is nothing to lose but grief

That imposition blights my quest
It does so to many others
Enters like an unwelcome guest
Impose its will, my life smothers

Out of the question, submission!
I accept nothing of its kind
Chains of this human condition?
No, I want to bring brighter mind

Be Kind

I offer kindness and concern
To all in the nature of love
I expect the same in return
In this the world in peace can live

For there will be no need for wars
No need for complex weaponry
No one suffering mental scars
No one homeless, alone, lonely

No child malnourished, miserable
No one in conflicting turmoil
No families vulnerable
Respect for life on our earth's soil

Then take up kindness, compassion
In the nature of truest love
Receive the same satisfaction
In this all the peoples will live

What kind of Education?

Civility is my education
To all nations whatever be their size
In a kindness and in a compassion
For the rich, for the poor, foolish or wise

For the bereaved losing their loved ones dear
Pity for those of arrogance possessed
Who scoff at kindness of others, so clear
Their fullness of help to all those distressed

The refugees fleeing persecution
For the starving and for the meek and mild
For the homeless seeking a solution
Shelter for brother, sister, parent, child

For our labours some kind, peaceful conquest
For wisdom to be found in words of grace
For the multitude of the dispossessed
For the survival of the human race

Forces Unseen

Happenings around me unseen
Many pictures to my eyes gleam
In nature's open secret scene
The myriads of beauties teem

In life-giving forces unseen
And out from the universe stream
Force happenings I could not dream
New life forms in multiple ream

Light traversing eternity
Across the galaxies so vast
I can view and think as empty
Space, what? Think, is it then so cast?

Can unseen forces be within?
This empty space, that it may teem
With living energies therein
With so many forces unseen

Whatever I do

For everything in life I then can do
For every journey I venture to make
For everyone I should meet as I go
For every action I take or don't take

For things I do and things I do not do
For when I should or when I should not do
For all the goodness I should then do
For all of the harm I should then so do

For to be wary of what I so pray
For the action that follows on from thought
For what follows on from thought that I say
For truth wrestled from untruth I have fought

Far better to think many thoughts of good
Far better to do an action of good
Far better to go on a venture good
Far better to be! And just to be! Good

To Think Freely

To be on a spiritual path
Making progress on my own path
So looking at those full of wrath
Are they on a similar path?

I must then truly make a stand
In ways such as I understand
Without thinking I be so grand
In life's way I make my own stand

In harmony, a true seeing
Myself in my clearer ways
On paths, those of noble being
Their good advice in myself stays

In my destiny as it will
In spirit free, in clarity
On noble path, enlightened still
In mind of true sincerity

The Heart Centre

Can we make it be so without too much of fuss?
That Britain be now the heart centre of the world
Can we be people so kind and so generous?
Can Britons open up and be that to the world?

To try to bring this about I must think, so act
In such a courageous and loving sought of way
To be free of selfishness, free to counteract
So much evil and to cast it out of my way

Let me go in good-will and so much loving care
Be in a mental state so to bring this about
Puzzled, I understand not why I stand and stare
If I have something wonderful to shout about

For whatsoever I give so shall I receive
Glorious to make the world a happier place
With such a love around us, a peace to conserve
Where all peoples can live in harmonious grace

The Tides

There doth flow the blue tidal seas
Ever the moon doth pull on them
There doth ebb the blue tidal seas
Ever the moon doth loosen them

To and fro to high and to low
To sea shallow and to sea deep
To ebb and to flow high and low
In constant movement calm and steep

So moves in full our planet blue
Circling our star, each day be new
Bathing in a warm sunlit hue
The rhythm of life doth shine through

The heart of this planet of ours
Universal time, pulsating
With a life in colourful hours
Expectations satisfying

Journey Back to Sanity

Here then so I go, now and then
Forever I go to and fro
So off the rails I do go then
Straight off the rough road so narrow

My thoughts then being wobbly things
Wasteful work and misery brings
Many hilarious doings
And many hilarious things

It is all part of my growing
This sane steadying of my nerves
To a balance I am sowing
Trying to cut out all the curves

To the straight and narrow I reach
Back to the path life is giving
The normality I did breach
In my growing, in my living

Dreams of Summerland

In the dark of mid-winter deep
In frosty cold of ice and snow
Life does slowly move, half-asleep
Where weak sunlit land gives pale glow

Spring sunshine, weakly promising
Lighting fresh life on barren land
Sun on snow, uncompromising
Ever budding trees appear grand

On ever brighter sunlit glades
Flowering flowers in meadows sweet
Pure sparkling rivers, sunlit shades
Dancing on beaming colours greet

All around the sound of nature
A hazy sight of happiness
A tranquillity of nurture
In scenes of heavenly gladness

Living my Life

Life is not what I may possess
It's what I can give to others
To play my part I must confess
Playing intentions with honours

My thoughts of being capable
Without any mischiefs concede
My intentions honourable
It being the way to succeed

I do not need thought of reward
To fill my own greedy pocket
I need to ever move forward
And of love in my heart, fill it

In the world I make my own way
Far better with someone I love
Both on the same loving pathway
Seeking together, heights above

Vain Ambitions

Pursuit of vain ambitions can destroy
All of my doings and good intentions
All of the things I then try to employ
To fulfil my earnest destinations

Ambitions in pursuit of my valour
Ambitions in pursuit of vanity
Ambitions of unproductive nature
Ambitions in pursuit of jealousy

These and many more thwart my very life
They take away my very consistence
As I pursue them destruction will thrive
So then to blight my very existence

I am not free then to do things jolly
My living of life is not then my own
I need to rid myself of such folly
I have truly reaped what I have then sown

What is Free

The wind blows on me, it is free
Rain falls from the sky, it is free
Sunshine gives me warmth, it is free
I look at blue sea, it is free

The light of the day, it is free
The dark sacred night, it is free
Bright moonshine in clouds, it is free
A blowing cloud roaming, it is free

Birds of the air, they should be free
Fish of the seas, they should be free
Mammals on land, they should be free
Human beings, they should be free

Creatures in cages are not free
Innocents caged who are not free
Caught for human research, Not free
Experimented on. Not free

Humanities Duty of Care

To those poorly and of ill-health
To those sadly fallen from grace
To those poor and of much less wealth
To those sadly gone without trace

To those broken and in despair
To those of whose actions destroy
To those crying and lacking care
But those whose good actions employ

To take on burdens of the poor
To guide children's education
To help the injured and the sore
Guide their chosen destination

To exceed divine excellence
To practise, to learn and to train
To achieve, with much persistence
Being key to success and gain

The Essence of Wisdom

Hearts of men wither with desire
Want and ignorance aren't phantoms
As hope is as hollow as fear
And both hope and fear are phantoms

That arise from myself-thinking
When I do not see self as self
What do I have then of fearing
See the world as much as myself

If I open myself to loss
I can then accept it complete
I am truly at one with loss
My responses will be complete

Love the world as my very self
Just realise where I come from
Then care for all things as myself
This, the true essence of wisdom

Things to Teach

To have patience and compassion,
simplicity
Because all of beings have emotions
alike
And in my actions and thinking,
simplicity
Keeping patient with friends and enemies
alike

And so, being with the way things are in the
world
In my thoughts and emotions, being very
still
I can reconcile with all beings in the
world
I can love and lead without imposing my
will

I can give birth to peace and welfare
solutions
Benefit to have all without possessing
it
Of my doings without any
expectations
Leading the world and not trying to control
it

All my hopes and fears arise from thinking of
self
And when I stop seeing my very self as
self
I can give compassion to all and my own
self
Being able of seeing the world as
myself

The Universal Intelligence

We are all very much a part of this
concept
Everyone is so without any
exception
Things, the physical body we can touch and
feel
The consciousness of which we are only
aware

This intelligence surrounds our very
planet
It is the life force that sustains all and
everything
We can then at this stage of ourselves
evolving
Only to having a slight awareness of
it

For it has been, is now and will be all life
forms
Our life forms past and present like earth, sea
and sky
And will be so in the ever coming
future
For it has so been there since beginningless
time

It's not a man in the sky people call a
God
Mankind is fast outgrowing such a God
concept
No worship for it, it's love that only
matters
Can it be that all of mankind is
evolving?

The Wisdom of Intuition

The wisdom of intuition
As a concept it can't be grasped
It's in the human condition
It's always there, it's never lapsed

It's been there from the beginning
There now and will be forever
Will never be disappearing
It's always in use forever

Most aren't even aware of it
Do not even know it is there
Can't even grasp the truth of it
Let alone of it being there

But to those of us who do know
Of this truth, it is wise to teach
But not to doing just for show
Our own bravado, I beseech

A Supreme Virtue

Simplicity, patience and compassion
Simplicity in action and thinking
Doing without expectation
Possession without really possessing

Patient with friends and with enemies still
All in accordance with the way things are
Love people without imposing my will
Reconcile on our celestial star

Awaken peace within my very heart
Giving birth and nourishing all the team
Lead but not try to control from the start
Is this then really the virtue supreme?

Love the world as myself in everything
Just realise where I truly come from
Then I can surely care for everything
Is this then the true essence of wisdom?

Eat, Drink and be Merry

Eat and drink and then be merry
For when tomorrow comes, we die
The mentality of many
Late for some to regret, to sigh

Yet mankind has overcome scars
In its long, bloody histories
It has risen from raging wars
Future dawns to new strategies

Each new year brings to us some hope
That wisdom over foolishness
Should take control of man to cope
And prevail in togetherness

The world as one, one common cause
To breath, to think, to be alive
To take from the same common source
To save fragile earth, to survive

Love Thy Neighbour

If everybody so loved everybody
else
And then everybody else loved
everybody
Nobody would be hurting anybody
else
Everybody else would be hurting
nobody

There'd be no need in the world for
malnourishing
We would not see any of our loved ones
starving
There'd be no homeless ones unloved and
wandering
We would not want to see our loved ones
floundering

In bereavement there would be none left so
lonely
Everyone would have someone, all then would
belong
Everyone would then be cared for, to feel
homely
Everyone would be so loved, all would sing their
song

Happiness would then be seen and felt all
around
Love, hope and fellowship very secure and
sound
Loving progression all about us would
abound
Peace would then reign forever on sure solid
ground

Comment from the author.
So it seems that at the end of the day
There would appear to be no other way

Stonehenge to the Stars

The facets of humanity
Being as numerous as leaves
That blossom on full sanity
That enhancing mind far believes

That flowing of evolution
Thus creating great things of love
Not by the flow to destruction
But symbolic peace of the dove

Such is mankind's intelligence
Wisdom mixed with bursts of folly
Inventions of their negligence
Grieving to formations sorry

Be these flights of thinking notions?
From the ancient's building of stones
Mystical symbol formations
Circles, portal doorways and crowns

Be these mankind's thinking cradles?
The in good times of evolving
Take to starward very stable
Facing problems in the solving

When we can be truly enhanced
Fit minded to take on the stars
And by the planets be entranced
Can we learn from mankind's past scars?

Show some kind of civility
Without giving destruction to
Show the best of humanity
In those places we venture to

Develop better than we've ever done
On this, our poor, brave, earthly place
With wrong and catastrophy gone
We need to have a saving grace

Comment from the author.
The grace to forgive ourselves
and have no more wrong doings

A Way of Life

To practise its understanding
To understand ultimate truth
Investigate correct meaning
And in the way things are, have faith

To look at the world as myself
Look for harmony in myself
To love the world as in myself
Be content, simply be myself

Return to the source of being
Nothing is lacking within me
Take in all that I am seeing
Then the whole world belongs to me

All the things that are true and kind
Beauty, love, creativity
Joy, inner peace, beyond the mind
Arise in good activity

Dream or Nightmare

The days events in mind may creep
Not all may be as it may seem
Then as I go to bed to sleep
So as I go to bed to dream

In surprise or anxiety
Haunting my time of night sleeping
Showing vivid variety
Or gentle grace to my dreaming

But when I lay to sleep at night
It be best to think of things nice
Lest I drift off and in my fright
Suffer my greatest fall from grace

But all in all I then wake up
Moments later all fades away
I make a cup of tea to sup
And then get on with my nice day

Scary Nightmares

Are these then just the events of the day?
And of the brains mixed up connotations?
A release of tension stress in my way
Of worries and many tribulations

Of terrifying experiences
Or just a series of bad scary dreams
Can my mind play tricks on utterances
Reflect my daytimes pranks and foolish games

Can I then control my way of thinking?
Am I then not at peace myself within?
Subduing intellectual tinkling
Put it all to rest and let sleep begin

As soon on my waking they take their flight
Gone after a few brief moments it seems
On waking I get back to normal sight
The question is, "Do I learn from my dreams?"

Footprints in the Sand

I watched the footprints in the sand
To learn from these the paths to take
To think I'm on a journey grand
Those gone before did for my sake

Leave their prints for me to follow
All the way to their journey's end
Followers suffer less sorrow
And all those can be called a friend

They did leave their clear prints behind
So all can make of less mistakes
They did leave for all of mankind
A show of the courage it takes

They learnt from people gone before
Who learnt from venturers of past
In our memories of folklore
Histories footprints, shall they last?

Uplifting Blossoms

Colours all so bright and cheerful
Delicate petals big and small
Swaying in branches long and full
Stout, well rooted trees short and tall

Windy play, such a merry dance
Within swirling waves to and fro
Warm breezes true to style, their prance
In and out, up and down they go

In leaping breezes and showers
And with wind cascades of scent
Flowing from petals of flowers
Perfume lifting and heaven scent

Such peace and a tranquillity
Uplifting in their blossoming
Timeless giving of quality
Never failing in comforting

Why are Humans more able than Animals?

It is because of reasoning
ability
So much more advanced than that of the
animals
Theirs is one of instinctive
capability
Whilst ours is one of creative thinking
mammals

We have ability to rise with
persistence
To reasoning out of intricate
solutions
The difficulties in conditioned
existence
To be able to come to many
conclusions

We can inhabit various
environments
Surroundings where many a creature would
perish
We can survive the many suffering
ailments
We're presented with by nature, whom we
cherish

We're able to organise ourselves to
survive
With due consideration for one
another
And to all those humans themselves who bravely
strive
To have compassion and kindness grace each
other

Comment from the author.
Actions in the last verse put into practice
become immensely meaningful in our struggle
for survival and advancement

Printed in Great Britain
by Amazon

23433756R10037